ART FROM THROWAWAYS
Early Learning Activities That Promote Recycling Awareness

by Patty Claycomb
illustrated by Marilynn G. Barr

This book is dedicated with love to:
Robert Claycomb

Publisher: Roberta Suid
Copy Editor: Carol Whiteley
Senior Editor: Annalisa Suid
Production: Santa Monica Press
Educational Consultant: Sarah Felstiner

Entire contents copyright © 1995 by Monday Morning Books, Inc.
Other books in the Happy World series include:
Animal Friends (MM 2012) and
Friends from Around the World (MM 2013)

For a complete catalog of our products, please write to the address below:
P.O. Box 1680, Palo Alto, CA 94302

Monday Morning is a registered trademark of
Monday Morning Books, Inc.

ISBN: 1-878279-25-4

Printed in the United States of America

987654321

8.95

CONTENTS

INTRODUCTION

Art from Throwaways is filled with activities for creative crafts that can be made easily from recyclable items. By using them you will be scheduling fun projects for your students, while helping to clean up the planet!

Using materials normally headed for the garbage (milk cartons, cereal boxes, cardboard tubes, etc.), the activities in this book help children recycle while creating art: wearable art ("Wild West Vests"), art to decorate wall space ("Butterfly Swarm"), functional art ("Piggy Banks"), and more.

Each activity in *Art from Throwaways* begins with a "Teacher's Note" that gives you extra information about the subject of the project. For example, "Primitive Drawings" begins with a paragraph describing life during cave times. Following project information are materials and directions for creating the crafts. Finally, there is a "Book Link," usually a storybook that ties to the theme of the activity (occasionally, non-fiction books are listed).

Accompanying each project is a rebus-style set of instructions for you to duplicate and hand out to your students. The materials are listed on the top of the page (in picture form). The boxed instructions are all given in three picture steps, with the final project shown in the fourth square. Older children can create the crafts all by themselves. You can lead younger children through the crafts, following the simple step-by-step process.

The book is divided into four parts, based on the types of materials used. For example, chapter one is dedicated to paper products (bags, plates, cups, and so on). Each chapter begins with a fun poem or silly song that you can teach your students.

Encourage your students' creativity with the innovative projects in *Art from Throwaways*.

LETTER TO PARENTS

Dear Parents,

Our class is beginning a unit on making art from recycled materials. You can help us by saving specific items and sending them to school with your child.

We are in need of the following: paper products (bags, cups, and plates), dairy cartons (milk cartons, margarine and butter tubs, yogurt containers), boxes (cereal, shoe, and so on), and extras (cardboard tubes, empty cans, plastic lids, and meat trays).

You will be able to enjoy the creative art projects that your child makes with these materials. And you will be helping take care of the planet at the same time!

Thank you for your assistance.

Sincerely,

HELLO, MR. TREE!
(to the tune of "The Farmer in the Dell")

Hello, Mr. Tree,
Hello, Mr. Tree,
Hello, Mr. Leafy Tree,
What do you do for me?

I give you fruit to eat,
A shady place that's neat—
But if I bend and fold and sag
Then I'm a paper bag!

Hello, Mr. Tree,
Hello, Mr. Tree,
Hello, Mr. Leafy Tree,
What do you do for me?

I'm safe to hide a nest,
For any bird at rest,
But if you're on a picnic date
Then I'm a paper plate!

Hello, Mr. Tree,
Hello, Mr. Tree,
Hello, Mr. Leafy Tree,
What do you do for me?

I'm beautiful to see,
I'm more than just a tree—
And when you drink from paper cups
Be sure to think of me!

CHAPTER ONE: PAPER PRODUCTS

PRIMITIVE DRAWINGS

Teacher's Note:
Explain to your students that many thousands of years ago, there were no grocery or clothing stores. People hunted animals to feed, clothe, and care for themselves. All parts of the animals were used: the meat for food, the skin for clothing, the horns and bones for medicine. Nothing was ever wasted.

Materials:
Paper bags (one per child), scissors, crayons

Directions:
1. Have the children cut out one side from their paper bag, moving their scissors back and forth to make a wavy border.
2. Tell the children to pretend that their piece of paper is an animal skin, and provide crayons for the children to color or draw on their "skins."
3. When they have finished drawing, have the children crumple the "skins."
4. Show the children how to open the crumpled papers and then rub both sides together many times to give the pictures an old, weathered appearance. The paper will begin to feel as soft as leather!
5. Post the primitive drawings on an "Ancient Art" bulletin board. Encourage the children to look at the pictures and imagine what the world was like a long time ago.

Book Link:
• *Early Humans* edited by Phil Wilkinson (Knopf, 1989).
Show your students pictures from this Eyewitness Book about ancient peoples. You can also choose a few exciting excerpts to read to your class.

PRIMITIVE DRAWINGS

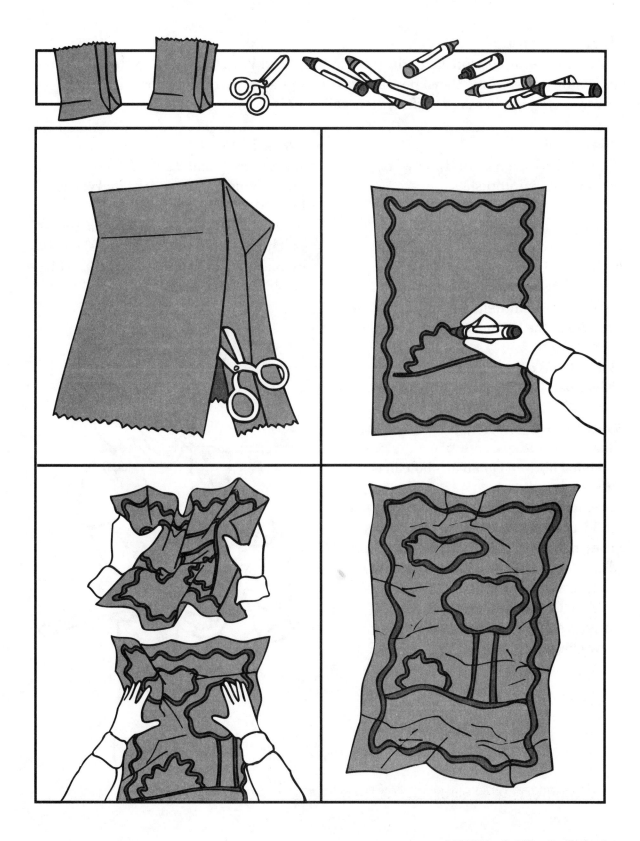

WILD WEST VESTS

Teacher's Note:
Have a lively discussion about the days in the "Wild West." Let the children brainstorm everything they know about cowboys and cowboy fashions: lassoing, covered wagons, herds of buffalo, "ten-gallon hats," cowboy boots, and so on.

Materials:
Paper bags (one per child), scissors, tempera paint, paintbrushes

Directions:
1. Have each child open up a paper bag and place it upside down. One of the larger sides should be facing the child.
2. Show the children how to cut from the middle of the bottom of the bag straight to the top crease.
3. Next, have them cut across the top. The paper bags will open up like vests. (You may want to make one first, to show children what the final project will look like.)
4. Help children cut an armhole in each side of their bags.
5. Provide tempera paint and brushes for children to use to decorate their vests. They might want to try to paint western designs (cacti, sheriff badges, lassoes, horses, and so on).
6. Once the vests have dried, stage a fashion show and let children wear their new clothes!

Book Link:
• *The Cowboy and the Black Eyed Pea* by Tony Johnston, illustrated by Warren Ludwig (Putnam's, 1992).
Farethee Well, the daughter of a Texas rancher, decides to test for a real cowboy by placing a pea under fifty saddle blankets!

WILD WEST VESTS

BUTTERFLY SWARM

Teacher's Note:
Butterflies are beautiful insects. Their good eyesight lets them move quickly from flower to flower. They use their long tongues to feed on nectar, water, and tree sap. Butterflies grow from an egg to a caterpillar to a chrysalis (in a cocoon) and finally to an adult butterfly. When they are caterpillars, they eat the most. Two caterpillars can eat one large plant!

Materials:
Paper bags (one per child), tempera paints in a variety of colors, paintbrushes, newsprint, scissors, tape

Directions:
1. Have the children cut out one large side from their paper bag.
2. Provide tempera paints and brushes for children to use to paint the outlines of large butterflies on the paper.
3. Help children cut out their butterflies.
4. Children can place their paper bag butterflies over newsprint (to protect tables from paint drips or spills) and paint the wings a variety of magnificent colors.
5. Once the butterflies have dried, tape them together on a wall. Bend the wings upward to make it look as if the butterflies are flying. Label the bulletin board "Butterflies Flutter By."
6. Have the children admire their beautiful swarm of butterflies!

Book Link:
• *Darkness and the Butterfly* by Ann Grifalconi (Little, Brown, 1987).
This is a beautiful story about a little girl who is afraid of the dark. A wise woman and a yellow butterfly help her face her fears. This captivating tale (with entrancing illustrations) will help your children to see the beauty of the night.

BUTTERFLY SWARM

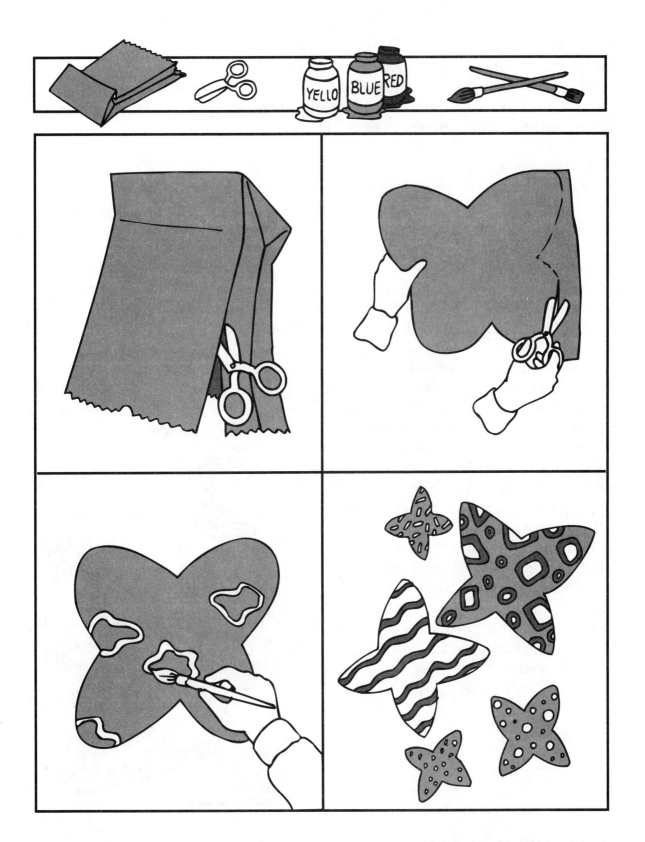

BABY DINOSAURS

Teacher's Note:
Ask the children if they have ever seen a dinosaur. Explain that dinosaurs lived on Earth before humans. Some ate plants, and others ate each other! Some dinosaurs flew, others walked on the land, and still others swam in the seas. Have the children imagine what dinosaurs looked like.

Materials:
Paper cups (one per child), pipe cleaners, tape, glue, cotton balls, tissue paper, tinfoil, Cheerios (optional)

Directions:
1. Give each child a paper cup and two pipe cleaners.
2. Have the children place the cups topside down.
3. Show the children how to tape one end of a pipe cleaner underneath the cup. (Most of the pipe cleaner will be sticking out.) Have the children bend this part up to form a long neck, then bend the top down to form a head.
4. Have the children tape one end of the second pipe cleaner under the other side of the cup to make the tail.
5. Children can use cotton balls, tissue paper, aluminum foil, Cheerios, and glue to make the hides (or skin) for their dinosaurs.
6. Once the glue has dried, have the children place their creatures on a table with a "Dinosaurs Rule!" label.

Option:
Draw a giant (5' x 3') dinosaur on a sheet of butcher paper. Provide a variety of tempera paints for children to use to paint the dinosaur. When each child has finished painting, have your students admire their beautiful "Rainbowsaurus."

Book Link:
• *Danny and the Dinosaur* by Syd Hoff (HarperCollins, 1958).
A little boy is surprised and pleased when one of the dinosaurs from the museum agrees to play with him.

BABY DINOSAURS

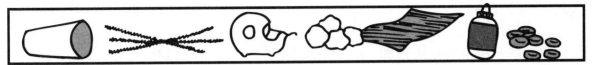

PENNY OWLS

Teacher's Note:
Owls have soft, flexible feathers that allow them to fly without making noise. Their eyes face forward, so they rotate their head to see around themselves. Owls have a "mask" around their eyes that is made from special flat feathers. These feathers direct sound toward the owls' ears. Owls live in nests abandoned by other birds rather than build nests of their own.

Materials:
Paper cups (one per child), feathers, glue, knife (for teacher's use only), pennies (three per child)

Directions:
1. Cut a slit in the upper half of each paper cup. (See illustration.)
2. Show the children how to slip a penny into the slit to make a beak.
3. Now the children can glue two pennies above the slits. These make the owls' eyes.
4. Provide glue and feathers for children to use to create colorful bodies for their owls.
5. When the owls have dried, the children can find a dark place in the classroom to keep their owls until they bring them home.

Book Link:
• *The Owl Who Became the Moon* by Jonathan London (Dutton, 1993). Readers travel through snow-covered, moon-lit mountains in this story; the beauty of the woods is entrancing. Throughout the train ride in the story, an owl appears and shines majestically in all his nocturnal beauty.

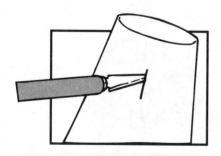

PENNY OWLS

©1995 Monday Morning Books, Inc.

OYSTER SURPRISE

Teacher's Note:
The oyster is a mollusk, a soft-bodied animal that produces an outer shell. It can withdraw into its shell for protection. The oyster attaches itself to rocks by a muscular foot. Pearls are formed when an object becomes embedded in the oyster's tissues. If the oyster does not expel it in a few days, it becomes covered with layers of "shell" material, and a pearl is born!

Materials:
Paper plates (two per child), crayons (including brown, gray, and cream), glitter, stapler, glue, marbles (one per child), green crepe paper streamers (optional)

Book Link:
• *The Walrus and the Carpenter* by Lewis Carroll, illustrated by Jane Breskin Zalben (Holt, 1986).
Read a few stanzas of this famous poem from the classic children's book *Alice's Adventures in Wonderland*.

Directions:
1. Have each child color the backs of two paper plates using only brown, gray, and cream colored crayons. These plates will be the outside shells of the oysters.
2. Place the rest of the crayons on the table and have the children color the inside of their plates.
3. Provide glue and glitter for children to use to decorate the insides of their plates.
4. Give each child a marble to glue to one of the glittery insides. This will be the oyster's pearl.
5. Staple each pair of oyster shells together so that the glittery sides are inside. Children can peek inside their oysters to see the colored inner shells and pearls.
6. Line the oysters up in a "seaweed" oyster bed you make from green crepe paper streamers. Remind children to share the surprise inside their oysters when they take them home.

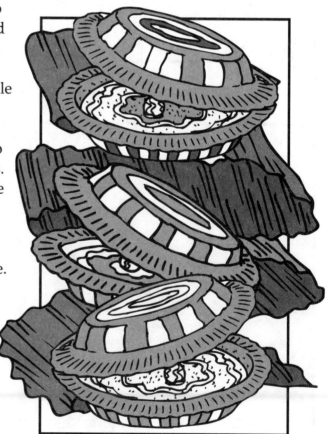

OYSTER SURPRISE

UFO SIGHTINGS

Teacher's Note:
Ask the children if they know what a UFO is. Some people say UFOs are aircraft that come from another planet. UFOs have been described as having many shapes and flashing colors. Ask the children who they think might be inside a UFO, and why one would visit Earth. Then ask them whether they would travel in a UFO if they had the chance.

Materials:
Paper plates (two per child), felt markers, sticky stars, pipe cleaners, stapler, tape

Directions:
1. Give each child two paper plates to color (on the outside). The children can draw windows, doors, colorful lights, and aliens!
2. Help children staple their two plates together. (The colored sides should be showing.)
3. Show children how to add an antenna. Each child can choose a colored pipe cleaner, bend an inch of it at one end, and tape this end over a stapled edge.
4. Now the UFOs are ready to take off! Have children zoom their UFOs around the room.

Book Link:
• *Space Case* by Edward Marshall, illustrated by James Marshall (Dial, 1980).
In this book, a friendly UFO visits Earth and makes friends with a boy. It visits his home and goes to school with him. Find out how hard it might be to hide a UFO!

UFO SIGHTINGS

TURTLE PETS

Teacher's Note:

Turtles are reptiles that have lived on Earth since the time of the dinosaurs! Their shell is their skeleton, which grows on the outside of their bodies. If you talk to a turtle, it won't look at you. If you pound on the ground, it will! Turtles pick up vibrations through the ground and through water. They will go to the same feeding area at the same time every day.

Materials:

Paper plates (two per child), green construction paper, scissors, felt markers, crayons (brown, green, and cream), tape

Directions:

1. Have the children draw lines going across the back of a paper plate with felt markers. Then have them draw lines going up and down. This makes the turtle shell design.
2. Provide crayons for children to use to color the grid design.
3. Show children how to cut a head and feet for their pet turtles from the green construction paper.
4. Have children tape on the head and feet. Then have them tape the two plates together. Now they each have a turtle pet to take home!

Book Link:

• *The Turtle and the Moon* by Charles Turner, illustrated by Melissa Bay Mathis (Dutton, 1991).
Turtle lives alone in the tall grass. Readers will go with him on his daily routines, but he has a problem. He has no one to play with. He does, however, notice the moon, which is always with him. The soft pastel pictures in this book are lovely!

TURTLE PETS

Moo Cow Moo

(to the tune of "Do You Know the Muffin Man?")

Oh, Mrs. Cow, how do you do?
Oh, Mrs. Cow, I do love you.
For making me a glass of milk,
I thank you, moo cow moo!

Oh, Mrs. Cow, how do you do?
Oh, Mrs. Cow, I do love you.
For butter that I like to spread,
I thank you, moo cow moo!

Oh, Mrs. Cow, how do you do?
Oh, Mrs. Cow, I do love you.
For yogurt I can eat with bread,
I thank you, moo cow moo!

Oh, Mrs. Cow, how do you do?
On green, green grass, you chew and chew.
For making many things I use,
I thank you, moo cow moo!

CHAPTER TWO: DAIRY CARTONS

TREASURE BOXES

Teacher's Note:
Ask the children what they think is inside a treasure box. (Treasure, of course!) A treasure box holds things that people really like. These boxes can be beautiful or ordinary. Ask the children what they would like to keep in a treasure box, and where they would keep it.

Materials:
Milk cartons (one per child), a knife (for teacher's use only), glue, scraps of construction paper, sticky stars, cotton balls, stickers, tape, yarn, tissue paper, pretty pictures cut from magazines

Directions:
1. Cut away one side from each milk carton. Tape the peaked sides together, and give one to each child.
2. Have the children lay their milk carton on the table. The cut-out side should be facing upward.
3. Explain to the children that their milk cartons will become treasure boxes. They can decorate their boxes in any way that they'd like using glue, sticky stars, cotton balls, stickers, yarn, tissue paper, magazine cutouts, and so on.
4. Let the children take their treasure boxes home to hold special prizes.

Book Link:
• *Captain Teachum's Buried Treasure* by Korky Paul and Peter Carter (Oxford University Press, 1991).
This book explains why Captain Teachum is considered to be the wickedest pirate around. Read this entrancing story and find out his three secrets and what his real treasure is.

TREASURE BOXES

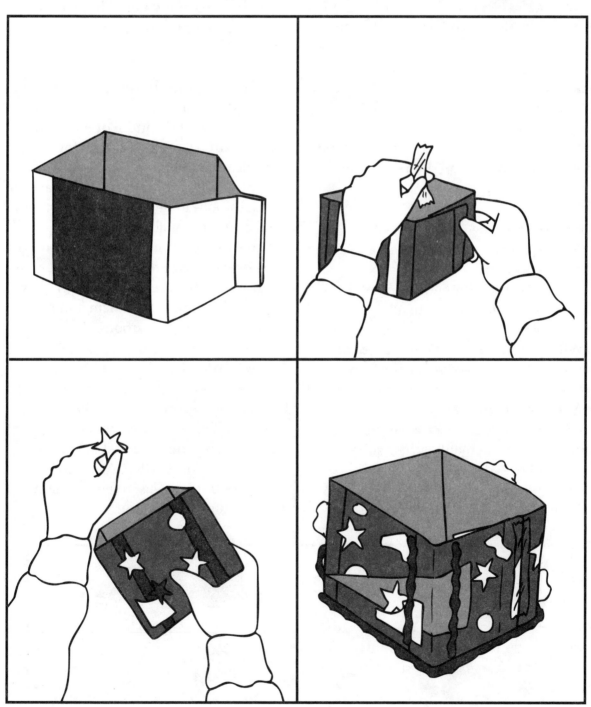

YELLOW SUBMARINES

Teacher's Note:
Ask the children if they know how a submarine is different from other boats. A submarine sinks below the surface of the water and comes back up. It is able to do this because it takes in water to help it sink, then pumps out water to help it float. A sub also has other special features. Sailors inside an underwater sub can see above the water by looking through a periscope.

Materials:
Milk cartons (one per child), knife (for teacher's use only), yellow paint, paintbrushes, colored construction paper, tape, blue crepe paper, colored pipe cleaners

Directions:
1. Cut out one side from each milk carton. Tape the peaked edges together, and give one to each child.
2. Provide yellow tempera paint and paintbrushes for children to use to turn their milk cartons into yellow submarines.
3. When the submarines have dried, place a variety of colored construction paper on the table. Children can choose a sheet to be the top of their submarines.
4. Show the children how to lay their sheet over the open top of their submarine, bend the edges down, and tape them.
5. Give each child a colored pipe cleaner periscope to poke through the middle of the construction paper. When the periscope touches the bottom of the submarine, children should bend the top of the pipe cleaner down.
6. Tape a strip of blue crepe paper across the classroom to be the top of the ocean. (Make sure it's at child height.)
7. Have the children hold their yellow submarines above their heads (and above the waves of the crepe paper sea.) They can slowly "submerge" them and move them around the classroom.

Book Link:
• *Submarines and Other Underwater Craft* by Harvey Weiss (Crowell, 1990).
This book explains how submarines work and what they do. The first submarine was called "The Turtle." Ask the children why they think it was given this name. Then read on to find out.

YELLOW SUBMARINES

PIGGY BANKS

Teacher's Note:
Ask some questions about piggy banks, such as, "What shape do you think a piggy bank is?" "What do you keep in a piggy bank?" "Why is a pig a good shape in which to keep many pennies?" "How do you get pennies out of a piggy bank?" "If you had money in a piggy bank, what would you want to buy with it?"

Materials:
Milk cartons (one per child), pink construction paper, scissors, felt pens, tape, a knife (for teacher's use only), pink tempera paint, paintbrushes, glue, pennies (one per child)

Directions:
1. Tape the peaked edges of the milk cartons together.
2. Provide pink tempera paint for children to use to paint their cartons. Let dry.
3. Show the children how to draw a pig face on a sheet of construction paper and then cut it out.
4. The children can then glue their pig faces on the side of their milk cartons.
5. Cut a small slit near the top of the carton. Give each child a penny to put in his or her piggy bank.

Book Link:
• *Oink* by Arthur Geisert (Houghton Mifflin, 1991).
This is an adorable wordless picture book. While mama pig takes a nap, her eight piglets sneak off. Follow their mischief as they try to find something to eat. What do you think happens when mama pig wakes up and finds her babies are missing? How loud do you think she can yell? OINK!

PIGGY BANKS

LADYBUG, LADYBUG

Teacher's Note:
Ladybugs are red-shelled beetles with black spots. They can be found in forests, by ponds, in gardens and fields, and under leaves. Some beetles like to live on water or under rocks, but the ladybug prefers to live near plants. It eats aphids, which are tiny green insects that are harmful to plants. For this reason, the ladybug is a friend to gardeners and farmers. Some people consider ladybugs to be good luck.

Materials:
Margarine or soft butter containers (one per child), glue, tape, paintbrushes, pipe cleaners, red and black crepe paper (cut into 3" strips), green construction paper, scissors

Directions:
1. Have the children turn the butter containers upside-down and brush glue over the bottom and sides.
2. Provide red and black crepe paper strips for children to crunch into balls and glue to the containers. They should continue crunching and gluing until their containers are covered. (The black represents dots on the red beetle shell.)
3. Show the children how to bend the pipe cleaners and tape them to the underside of the ladybugs to make antennae.
4. Cover a table with large green leaf cutouts. Have the children set their ladybugs on the leaves where they can eat aphids and be happy. Later, children can take their lucky beetles home with them.

Book Link:
• *Ladybug Ladybug* by Ruth Brown (Dutton, 1988).
Ladybug believes that her house is on fire and tries to find her way home. Most of the animals she meets along the way don't help her, but one does. Have the children pretend that they are flying with the ladybug over the countryside to reach her home.

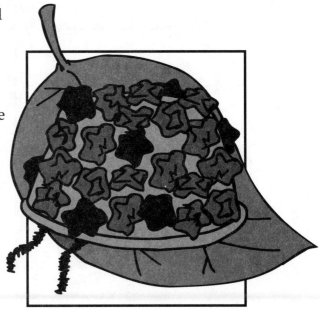

LADYBUG, LADYBUG

BEAUTIFUL CATERPILLAR

Teacher's Note:
It is always exciting to find a caterpillar! Once the caterpillar hatches from its egg, it is very hungry. It eats, grows bigger, sheds its skin (called "molting"), eats more, and continues to repeat this process. Finally, it spins a cocoon around itself. A cocoon protects the caterpillar while it becomes a butterfly.

Materials:
Margarine or soft butter containers (one per child), masking tape, clear tape, marker, two pipe cleaners, glue, tissue paper, cotton balls, construction paper scraps, glitter, yarn

Directions:
1. Give each child a butter container to make into a single section of a long caterpillar.
2. Provide cotton balls, construction paper scraps, glitter, glue, and yarn for children to use to decorate their caterpillar segment. They should try to make their caterpillar as unique as possible.
3. Print each child's name on a piece of masking tape and label the inside of each section. (This will insure that children find their own segment to take home.)
4. Tape the finished parts together at the bottom.
5. Choose one caterpillar section to be the head and tape two pipe cleaners at the top for the antennae.
6. Wind the caterpillar along a bookshelf or table top. Change its location often, and let children try to find it. When you are finished with it, take the caterpillar apart and let the children take home their own decorated containers.

Book Link:
• *Caterpillar Caterpillar* by Vivian French (Candlewick, 1993).
Grandfather shows his granddaughter the best way to learn about caterpillars. The reader, along with the granddaughter, learns interesting and uncommon facts about caterpillars. This story offers a great mix of fiction and nonfiction.

BEAUTIFUL CATERPILLAR

PEACEFUL HARBOR

Teacher's Note:
A sailboat is powered by the wind, instead of a motor. The main sail is usually a triangle, and is attached to the mast. The mast is a long pole in the middle of the boat. The boom is a shorter pole that supports the bottom of the sail. It is attached horizontally to the mast, a few feet above the boat deck.

Materials:
Butter containers (one per child), pipe cleaners, crayons, scissors, tape, yarn, tempera paint, paintbrushes, white construction paper (cut into 6"-long triangle sails), string

Directions:
1. Provide tempera paints and brushes for children to use to paint their butter containers. These will be their sailboats.
2. As the sailboats dry, give each child a triangle "sail" to decorate with crayons.
3. Give each child a pipe cleaner to bend at the base and tape to the middle of his or her sailboat. (This is the mast.)
4. Show children how to cut a second pipe cleaner in half and twist this around the mast. (This is the boom.)
5. Now children are ready to tape the sail to the mast.
6. Use a length of string to make a large circle on the rug. (Leave the ends of the circle open.) This will be the peaceful harbor for the boats, and the opening is the channel that leads to the ocean.
7. Let the children sail their boats slowly through the channel.

Book Link:
• *The Lady with the Ship on Her Head* by Deborah Nourse Lattimore (Harcourt Brace, 1990).
This is a wonderful fantasy story about Madame Pompenstaur, who wants to win the Best Headdress Award at the ball. She goes to the beach, puts a few shells in her hair, and a tiny sailing ship sails onto her head!

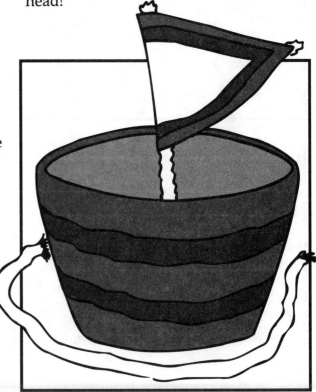

PEACEFUL HARBOR

TELEPHONE TALK

Teacher's Note:
Discuss the telephone as a means of communication: people can use one to talk to someone across the street or around the world. Ask the children if they know what to say when they answer a telephone. Practice by making "ringing" noises and then pointing to different children to "answer" the phone.

Materials:
Large paper plates and yogurt containers (one of each for each child), yarn, stapler, scissors, crayons, black felt pen, stickers, knife (for teacher's use only)

Directions:
1. With the black felt pen, copy the number sequence of a telephone onto each paper plate. (You may want an aide to help.)
2. Provide crayons and stickers for children to use to color and decorate their paper plate phones.
3. Cut two small holes at the bottom of each yogurt container.
4. Help each child thread a length of yarn through the holes and tie a knot at the bottom of the container.
5. For each child, staple the loose end of the yarn to the plate.
6. Now the children are ready to use their telephones. Have them sit on the rug. They can take turns dialing each other's numbers and pretending to talk to the person at the other end. You can also dial each child, one at a time, and ask questions.

Book Link:
• *Dial-A-Croc* by Mike Dumbleton, illustrated by Ann James (Orchard, 1991). Vanessa has a great idea for a way to make money using a telephone. Children will be interested in how she talks a crocodile into working with her.

TELEPHONE TALK

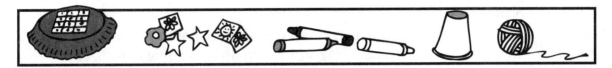

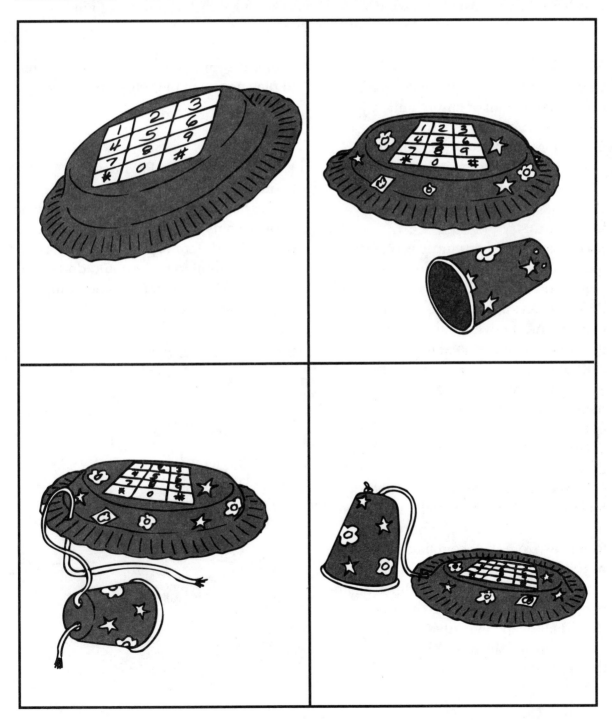

DROP THE PENNY

Teacher's Note:
Ask the children if they like playing games, and, if so, why. Possible answers: "You spend time with your friends," or "You learn to do something new." Ask which games they like to play and why. Then ask them if they can think of what a game called "Drop the Penny" would involve.

Materials:
One empty container per child (milk cartons cut in half or empty butter, yogurt, or sour cream containers), glue, tissue paper (cut into squares), glitter, cotton balls, construction paper scraps, pennies (one per child)

Directions:
1. Give each child an empty container to decorate. The children can use tissue paper, construction paper, glitter, cotton balls, and so on to decorate the sides of the containers however they want to. (The opening must be left alone.)
2. When all of the containers are finished (and dry), have the children place them on the rug.
3. Give each child a penny. Have the children stand directly over their containers.
4. Challenge the children to try to drop their pennies into their containers. As an option, they can kneel on the rug a few feet away from their containers and try to pitch their pennies into their containers. (The containers should all be lined against a wall in this case, and the children should all be the same distance away from them. The children should not be throwing the pennies toward each other at any time.)

5. Brainstorm other ways for the children to play games with their pennies and containers.

Book Link:
• *Benny's Pennies* by Pat Brisson (Doubleday, 1993).
Benny has five new pennies. Everyone he knows wants him to spend the pennies on something different. Ask the children what they think Benny should do with his pennies. Brightly colored paper sculptures make interesting illustrations!

DROP THE PENNY

HERMIT CRABS

Teacher's Note:
A hermit crab is born with a strong instinct for survival. When it outgrows its shell it looks for an abandoned one to move into. It lives in this shell until it grows too big for it, and then moves again. The hermit crab has eyes that stick up on stalks away from its body. When its body is hidden under the sand, its eyes pop up so it can see without being seen.

Materials:
Yogurt containers (one per child), hole punch, glue, colored yarn (cut into 2' strips), scissors, blue butcher paper, paintbrushes, pipe cleaners (cut into 4" strips), gold star stickers, tan construction paper

Directions:
1. Help the children punch four holes, side by side, at the top of their yogurt containers. Then have them turn the containers upside down to make a hermit crab shell.
2. Have the children push an end of a pipe cleaner into one of the holes. Show them how to twist the pipe cleaner end around the remaining portion so that it sticks out of the cup (see illustration). (They will do this with the remaining pipe cleaners and holes.) These are the legs of the hermit crabs.
3. Provide glue and paintbrushes for children to use to cover the surfaces of their containers. The children can now choose a colored length of yarn and wind it around their yogurt containers.

4. Spread a blue sheet of butcher paper on a table for children to place their completed crabs on. Label the paper "Terrific Tide Pool!" and decorate it with circular construction paper cutouts (for sand dollars) and gold star stickers (for starfish).

Book Link:
• *Looking for Crabs* by Bruce Whatley (HarperCollins, 1993).
This story follows a family that is looking for crabs at the beach. The children will discover the answer to the mystery of why this family can't find any crabs.

HERMIT CRABS

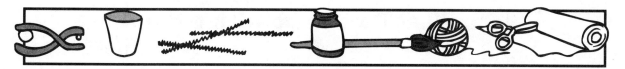

Oh, What Do You Do with a Box?

(to the tune of "100 Bottles of Pop on the Wall")

Oh . . .
What do you do with a box (a box),
What do you do with a box?
You stand on a box to pet an ox,
That's what you do with a box (a box)!

Oh . . .
What do you do with a box (a box),
What do you do with a box?
You throw in your pair of dirty socks,
That's what you do with a box (a box)!

Oh . . .
What do you do with a box (a box),
What do you do with a box?
You collect a lot of bugs and rocks,
That's what you do with a box (a box)!

Oh . . .
What do you do with a box (a box),
What do you do with a box?
You hide your head with the chicken pox,
That's what you do with a box (a box)!

CHAPTER THREE: BOXES

FRIENDLY ROBOTS

Teacher's Note:
Have the children brainstorm answers to the question "What is a robot?" Some robots can perform human tasks. Some are even built to look like people. Ask the children what they would want their own personal robot to do for them. Ask if they would like it to make their bed, or make them cookies.

Materials:
Cereal boxes (one per child), glue, scissors, paper towel rolls, construction paper scraps, buttons, glitter, pipe cleaners, sponges, paper cups, paper plates, tissue paper, cotton balls, aluminum foil, small boxes

Book Link:
• *Robot* by Jan Piénkowski (Delacorte, 1981).
This pop-up book features a family of robots. A different family member pops up on each page! There is also a robot dog, and robot pictures on the walls.

Directions:
1. Tell the children that they will be making friendly robots. Give each child a cereal box to use for the main body.
2. Provide a variety of the objects listed above for children to glue to their robot body for arms, legs, eyes, buttons, control panels, antennae, and so on.
3. When the robots have been assembled, have each child sit with his or her friendly robot in a circle on the floor.
4. Ask each child, in turn, to tell the robot's name and what it is programmed to do.
5. Have the children "robot walk" around the classroom, with stiff arms and legs. Remind them to wind each other up if they start to slow down!

FRIENDLY ROBOTS

TV WEATHERPERSON

Teacher's Note:
Ask if your students have seen weather reports on television. Describe a weather forecast for children who have not seen one. Then ask how your students might find out about the weather if they didn't have a television. Have everyone look out a window (or go outside). Now your students can report what the actual weather is (with more accuracy than many professional forecasters)!

Materials:
Cereal boxes (one per child), white construction paper, tape, crayons, pipe cleaners, buttons, glue

Directions:
1. Have the children brainstorm ideas for a weather picture. Their pictures could feature a rainy or sunny day, snow, clouds, hail, fog, wind, lightning, and so on.
2. Provide white construction paper and crayons for children to use to draw their own weather pictures.
3. Children can tape their finished pictures to the fronts of their cereal boxes.
4. Show children how to tape two pipe cleaners to the top of their cereal boxes for TV antennae. They can pretend to adjust the antennae for a clear picture!
5. Children can glue buttons to the sides of their cereal boxes for on/off switches and tuning knobs.
6. Now the children can sit with their televisions on the rug. Each child, in turn, can pretend to be a weatherperson and describe the forecast shown in his or her picture.

Book Link:
• *Cloudy with a Chance of Meatballs* by Judi Barrett, illustrated by Ron Barrett (Atheneum, 1978).
The people in the town of Chewandswallow don't need food stores because of their unusual weather: the sky drops food everyday. But this ends up causing some trouble, especially when the sky drops giant meatballs!

TV WEATHERPERSON

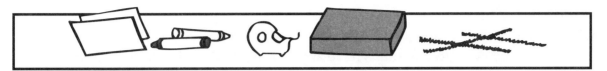

FLOWER GARDEN

Teacher's Note:
Ask the children what they would want to plant in their own private garden. Then ask if they think that gardens have any enemies. (They do!) Gardens can be damaged by harsh weather, snails, certain insects, and hungry rabbits. (Remember Peter Rabbit in Mr. McGregor's garden?)

Materials:
Cereal boxes (one per child), pipe cleaners, felt pen, brown construction paper, pastel construction paper and tissue paper cut into scraps, cotton balls, glue, tape, flower seeds, a knife (for teacher use only)

Directions:
1. Cover a large side of each cereal box with brown construction paper and tape in place. Make a box for each child in the class, and print each child's name on his or her box.
2. Poke a few holes, with a sharp knife, through the brown paper. Let each child drop a few flower seeds in the holes of his or her "garden" box.
3. Place the glue, paper scraps, pipe cleaners, and cotton balls on the table for children to use to make colorful flowers. They can glue the different papers into interesting designs, add a pipe cleaner stem, and a cotton ball center. Encourage them to make many beautiful flowers to grow in their gardens.
4. When the flowers are finished, the children can place one in each of the holes in their flower gardens.
5. Line the gardens together to make one large flower garden!

Book Link:
• *Planting a Rainbow* by Lois Ehlert (Harcourt, 1988).
This book shows you, step by step, how to plant a beautiful garden. The large colorful illustrations bring this book to life. The colors are so striking that they will make you want to smell the flowers! This book will encourage your children to appreciate the beauty of nature.

FLOWER GARDEN

SUPER STORES

Teacher's Note:
Ask the children if they have ever been to a store. If so, have them describe their experiences, prompting them with questions, such as, "Was the store in a mall, along a street, or near your house?" "What kind of things were sold in this store?" Then ask them to pretend that they each own a store, and ask them what types of items they would like to sell.

Materials:
Cereal boxes (one per child), colored construction paper, crayons, glue, scissors, a variety of pictures cut from magazines

Directions:
1. Children can choose a sheet of colored construction paper for their storefronts.
2. Provide crayons for children to use to add a front door and windows.
3. Children can glue their storefronts to the sides of their cereal boxes.
4. Provide an assortment of pictures cut from magazines for children to glue to their storefronts for merchandise.
5. When the stores are finished, line them up side by side to make a business area in a miniature city. If you'd like, label the city after your own town or school.

Book Link:
• *Moving to Town* by Mattie Lou O'Kelley (Little, Brown, 1991).
In this story, the colorfully detailed paintings help show a family that moves from the town to the city. The children in this family are excited to explore their new home, and also the large variety of new stores. Notice the difference between the town and city environments. Have the children try to find a horse in the city.

SUPER STORES

MOUSE HOUSES

Teacher's Note:
A mouse is a small rodent with gray, black, or white fur. It has rounded ears and a hairless tail. Ask the children if they know what kind of noise a mouse makes (SQUEAK!). There are jumping mice, pocket mice, field mice, and house mice. Mice who live in houses make their homes in walls.

Materials:
Shoe boxes (one per child), scissors, felt pens (black), glue, cotton balls, yarn (cut into 2" strips), small circles cut from felt, a variety of pictures cut from magazines, a knife (for teacher use only)

Book Link:
• *Cathedral Mouse* by Kay Chorao (Dutton, 1988).
A mouse leaves the security of a pet store and searches for a real home. He finds himself in a beautiful cathedral!

Directions:
1. Place the shoe boxes upside down. Draw a mouse-shaped door on each one and cut out.
2. Place the yarn strips, cotton balls, and glue on the table for the children to use to make mice to live in their mouse houses. They can glue a piece of yarn to one end of a cotton ball, glue on two felt ears up at the other end, and draw two eyes and a nose below the ears.
3. Next, the children can add furniture to their mouse houses with pictures cut from magazine pages. Have the children turn their mouse houses over and glue the pictures into the houses (upside down, so that the pictures will be right-side up for the mice)!
4. When the pictures have dried, have the children turn their mouse houses back so that the doors are in the right places. They can sit their little mice by the doors.
5. When it's time for children to take their mouse houses home, they can turn them back over and place their mice inside.

MOUSE HOUSES

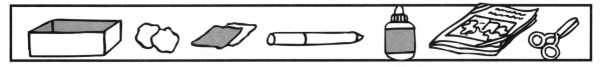

BEACH BOXES

Teacher's Note:
Ask the children to brainstorm reasons why people are attracted to the beach. Possible answers: to visit the ocean, to relax in the warm weather, to hunt for seashells, to go fishing. Ask the children to think of things they might find at a beach. Possible answers: people, lawn chairs, beach balls, beach towels, dried seaweed, sand crabs, smooth rocks, and tide pools.

Materials:
Shoe boxes (one per child), rocks, sand, black felt pen, blue crayons, glue, scissors, travel magazines (with pictures of beaches), seashells (optional)

Directions:
1. Have the children color one side of their boxes blue.
2. Fill each shoe box halfway with sand. Each child now has his or her own beach and ocean.
3. Place scissors and magazines on the table. The children can cut out pictures relating to the beach.
4. The children can glue their beach pictures in their beach box. They can also place rocks they have hunted for.
5. As an option, purchase small seashells and pass them out for children to add to their beach boxes.
6. Label each child's box, for example, "Wendi's Beach Box."
7. These beach boxes can remind your students of how special the beach environment is!

Book Link:
• *Greetings from Sandy Beach* by Bob Graham (Kane/Miller, 1992).
Take your children on a beach vacation with the family in this book. Children will see what the family packs, and what they do once they reach the beach!

BEACH BOXES

BIRTHDAY CAKE

Teacher's Note:
Ask your children if they know what special day a birthday cake is used to celebrate. Then ask them, "If there are five candles on your birthday cake, how old are you?" Explain to the children that the day they were born was a very special day. Talk about what might have happened on that day! Possible answers: your mom and dad got very excited, relatives called or came to the hospital to see you.

Materials:
Shoe boxes (one per child), tempera paint, paintbrushes, a knife, straws, birthday wrapping paper

Directions:
1. Poke holes through the top of the box lids. These holes will hold the "birthday candle" straws.
2. Place the paints and paintbrushes on the table for everyone to paint a birthday cake box. The children should pretend that the paint is the frosting as they spread it on.
3. Now, place the straws on the table. The children can poke these "candles" through the holes at the top of the cake.

4. When all the birthday cakes have dried, have the children sit on the rug with their cakes and sing a round of "Happy Birthday to Us!"
5. Display these cakes on a table covered with "Happy Birthday" wrapping paper.

Book Link:
• *The Biggest Birthday Cake in the World* by Elizabeth Spurr, illustrated by Rosanne Litzinger (Harcourt, 1991).
In this story, the richest man in the world is also the fattest man in the world! He hires 100 cooks to bake him the biggest birthday cake ever. Read this fun tale and find out what happens when the man refuses to share his cake.

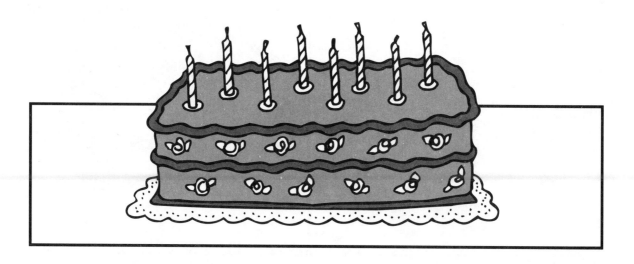

BIRTHDAY CAKE

UNDER THE OCEAN

Teacher's Note:
Ask the children the following question: "If you could look under the ocean, what do you think you would see?" The underwater world is full of brightly colored, fast-moving fish; slow-moving sea animals; and beautiful coral.

Materials:
Shoe boxes (one per child), blue tempera paint, paintbrushes, yarn (cut into 2" strips), tape, scissors, white construction paper, crayons

Directions:
1. Have each child paint the inside of his or her shoe box blue to represent the ocean.
2. Put the oceans in an area to dry. Place the remaining objects on the table.
3. Let children draw, color, and cut out their own fish and animal life.
4. When the children have finished creating their ocean life, they can tape each piece to the end of a yarn strip.
5. Stand the boxes on a long side, so the blue area is facing each child.
6. The children can then tape the free end of yarn pieces, without pictures, onto the top part of their box to create their own underwater views of the ocean!

Book Link:
• *Fish Fish Fish* by Georgie Adams (Dial, 1993).
This book introduces children to the idea that fish come in many different colors, shapes, and sizes. The fascinating pictures will make readers want to dive into the pages and experience the wonders of the sea!

UNDER THE OCEAN

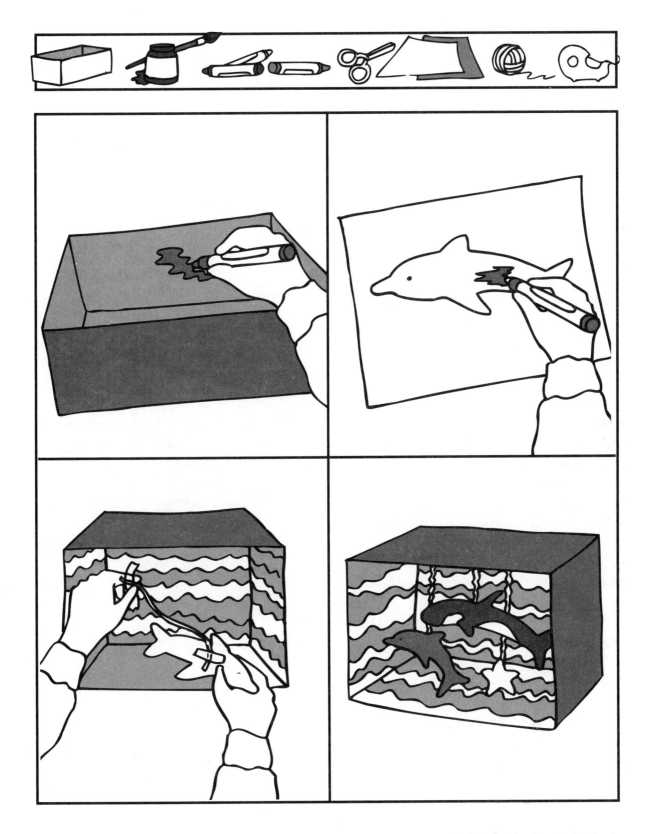

YOUR NEIGHBORHOOD

Teacher's Note:
Describe a neighborhood as an area where people live. It can be an area that has new homes, old homes, or mobile homes. Ask the children, in turn, to describe their neighborhoods and houses. Ask the children if they know the people who live around them, and explain that these people are their neighbors.

Materials:
Medium-sized boxes (one per child), white construction paper, crayons, glue, scissors, old magazines

Directions:
1. Cut white construction paper rectangles to cover one side of each of the boxes.
2. Place the boxes and crayons on the table. The children can give their house a paint job. They can color the front of their houses with crayons, adding a door, windows, and even a house number!
3. Now provide scissors and magazine pages so children can cut out pictures that might be seen in front of a house. Examples: trees, bushes, flowers, animals, gates, and people!
4. Have the children glue the pictures to the fronts of their houses.
5. Place all the houses together in a special area and have the children choose a name for their box neighborhood!

Book Link:
• *The House I Live In* by Isadore Seltzer (Macmillan, 1992).
This book shows the many different kinds of houses that are built in America, and the people who live in them. There are houseboats and farmhouses and many

types of neighborhood houses, as well as the surrounding environments. The pictures are colorful and detailed.

That's my house!

YOUR NEIGHBORHOOD

TOTEM POLE

Teacher's Note:

A totem is an animal, plant, or natural object that serves as the emblem of a clan or family. A totem pole is a post that is carved and painted with totems. Totems were built by some Native American tribes. Ask the children the following questions: "If you built a totem pole for your family, what would your totems look like?" "Would they look like your pets?"

Materials:

Large cardboard boxes (one per child), broad-tipped markers, tape, scissors, tempera paints, paintbrushes, colored construction paper, paper tubes, aluminum foil, tissue paper

Directions:

1. Give each child a large cardboard box to decorate to look like his or her own personal "totem."
2. Encourage the children to use their imaginations. They can cut out shapes from tissue paper or construction paper to tape to their boxes. They can use the aluminum foil, paper tubes, and tempera paints to make masks or animal faces on their boxes.
3. When the children have finished their totems, stack them on top of each other. Make one large totem pole, or two smaller ones.
4. Use the totem pole to decorate your classroom.

Book Link:

• *The Mountain Goats of Temlaham* by William Toye, photos by Elizabeth Cleaver (Oxford University Press, 1988). This Native American legend is set against pictures of totem poles and mountains. It shows how hunters become greedy and how the mountain goats seek revenge. In the story, a young boy named Raven Feather befriends a goat and grows into a wise teacher of his people. Almost every page shows a beautiful totem pole!

TOTEM POLE

What Am I?

I can bend in twists or spirals.
I can angle, hang, or turn.
I can be a stick, but leaner.
What am I?
(A pipe cleaner!)

I can crunch or clank or crinkle.
I can say, "Please drink me up!"
I am shiny, like a new van.
What am I?
(An aluminum can!)

Float me in a tub of water,
Add a sail, a piece of cloth.
Set me down, you know I'll stay.
What am I?
(A meat tray!)

I can be a bug's antennae.
I like leaning in your milk.
I can spy on any outlaw.
What am I?
(A drinking straw!)

CHAPTER FOUR:
EXTRAS

BABY ELEPHANTS

Teacher's Note:
An elephant is strong. It can uproot a tree with its trunk. It can also gently pluck an egg from a nest! An elephant is smart. It bumps its forehead against a tree trunk to make fruit fall. An elephant uses its long trunk to take a shower. Elephants care for each other. They will not leave a sick friend!

Materials:
Small cardboard tubes (one per child), gray construction paper, scissors, yarn, felt pens or crayons, tape

Directions:
1. Explain to the children that they will be making baby elephants.
2. Give each child a sheet of gray construction paper for the elephant's face. The children can use felt pens or crayons to draw on eyes and a mouth.
3. Have each child cut a length of yarn and tape one end below his or her elephant's eyes.
4. Show children how to run the yarn through a cardboard tube. Help children tape the tube over the yarn so that it is below the elephant's eyes. The tube should be sticking straight out!
5. Give each child a second sheet of gray construction paper, and show how to cut out large elephant ears by cutting a circle in half. The children can tape the ears to the sides of their pictures.
6. Post the elephant faces on a bulletin board labeled "Baby Elephants."

Book Link:
• *Tusk Tusk* by David McKee (Barron's, 1979).
All of the elephants in the world are either black or white. This story demonstrates what could happen if you want everyone else to look just like you. *Tusk Tusk* also explains how gray elephants came into the world.

BABY ELEPHANTS

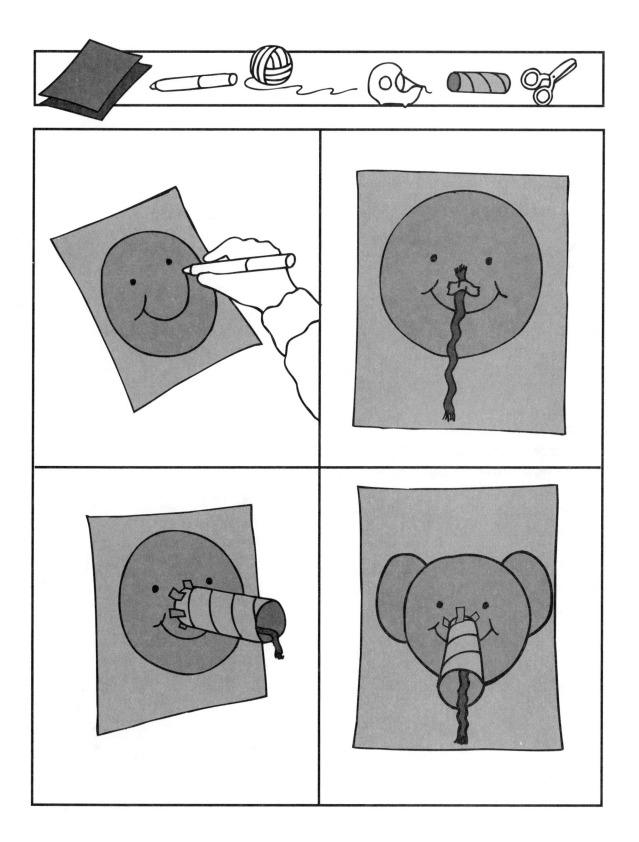

GRAVITY SLIDES

Teacher's Note:
Discuss gravity with your students. Gravity pulls everything towards the earth. Have the children jump up in the air. Then ask them, "Did you come down?" (Expect laughter.) Explain that gravity pulled them back down. Have the children bounce balls on the ground and ask them how many times gravity pulled the balls back down.

Materials:
Cardboard tubes and shoe boxes (one of each for each child), glue, tissue paper, construction paper, scissors, stickers, crepe paper, glitter, cotton balls, marbles

Directions:
1. Tell the children that they are going to make "Gravity Slides."
2. Give each child a shoe box (without the lid) to decorate using tissue paper, glue, construction paper, stickers, glitter, cotton balls, and crepe paper.
3. Give each child a cardboard tube to glue on one side of their finished box. The tube should be glued at an angle, so that a marble dropped from the top will travel through the tube and out into the box. This is a "Gravity Slide."
4. When the tubes have dried, give each child a marble to drop down his or her slide. Ask the children, "What pulls the marble through the tube?" (Gravity!)
5. The children can use other small objects (pebbles, dried beans, pennies) to drop down their gravity slides. (They can store these items in their boxes.)

Book Link:
• *Up and Up* by Shirley Hughes (Prentice-Hall, 1979).
In this wordless picture book, a little girl desperately wants to learn how to fly. She tries everything! Finally, she succeeds in flying, but is the flight real or imagined?

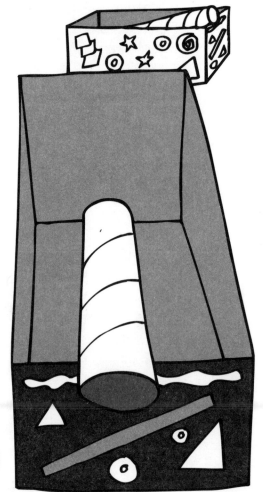

GRAVITY SLIDES

STRAW STATUES

Teacher's Note:
Ask the children to describe a statue. Then have them stand as still as statues! A statue is a form of art. It can be sculpted, modeled, carved, or cast in stone or wood. It can be large or small. It can be in the shape of a human (Michelangelo's David), an animal (Picasso's goat), or anything the artist imagines!

Materials:
Paper plates (one per child), glue, scissors, straws (cut into 2" strips), felt pen

Directions:
1. Give each child a paper plate and enough straw strips to build statues. The children can glue the straw strips in an upward direction, or make short, squat sculptures.
2. When the statues have dried, display them in a special area of the classroom.
3. Print the children's names on their plates.
4. Invite other classrooms to tour your statue art center. Your young artists can talk about their work as you lead guests through the "Straw Statue Museum."

Book Link:
• *All About Where* by Tana Hoban (Greenwillow, 1991).
This book offers a collection of photographs by Tana Hoban that revolves around concept words. Challenge the children to match each photograph with a concept word, such as, over, under, around, or behind. Children can find the animal in these photos that often looks like a statue.

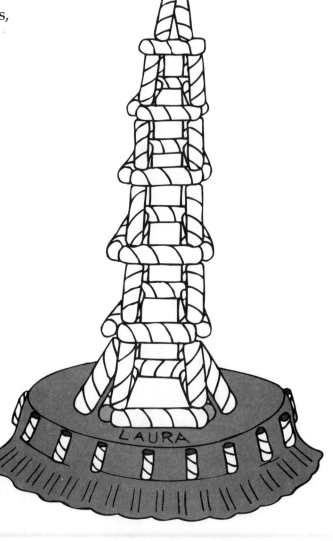

STRAW STATUES

CREATE-A-CAR

Teacher's Note:
Ask the children the question, "What does the word 'invention' mean?" An invention is something completely new. It did not exist anywhere else before—it is an original. Ask the children to try to think of something that has been invented. (Eight great All-American inventions are: Monopoly, television, Superman, King Kong, McDonalds, the Frisbee, Coca-Cola, and Levis.) Then ask them what items they hope to invent themselves.

Materials:
Meat trays (one per child), large marshmallows, glue, construction paper, aluminum foil, pipe cleaners, Popsicle sticks

Directions:
1. Place all of the materials on a table for children to use to invent new cars.
2. Children can glue the marshmallows to the bottom of their trays for wheels. (Be sure to have a few extra marshmallows on hand for snacking.)
3. Children can use the construction paper, foil, pipe cleaners, and Popsicle sticks to create their cars.
4. Have the children brainstorm names for their new cars. (You might tell them names of some existing cars to spark their imaginations, for example, Mustang, Galaxie, Spyder, Roadster, Fiesta, and Cougar.)
5. Place the cars on a table labeled "Inventors' Car Lot." Have the children look at the different designs. Invite the children to talk about their cars and the special features offered. (Cars might be able to fly, to talk to their owners, to drive themselves.)

Book Link:
• *The Great Big Car and Truck Book* by Richard Scarry (Golden Press, 1951). Each page of this book is filled with colorful pictures of different methods of transportation. Children can follow along with a family of pigs who are driving to the beach on vacation. Have the children look for the pigs on each page. (They can also find the cars that look like strange inventions, the doughnut car, for instance.)

CREATE-A-CAR

TRASH MACHINES

Teacher's Note:
Ask the children if they know what trash is made of. Trash is an accumulation of objects that we throw away. Ask the children what they think might happen if people continue to throw away more and more trash. Then brainstorm ideas for reducing trash. Perhaps we can recycle more, and use less.

Materials:
Jar lids and small boxes, paper cups and plates, glue, construction paper, sponges (cut into small pieces)

Directions:
1. Let children make "Trash Machines" using the materials listed above. They can glue the various objects together to assemble their machines.
2. While the children are inventing their machines, you can discuss what items the machines might have: wheels, an engine, a steering wheel, seats.
3. When the projects have dried, invite each child, in turn, to talk about his or her trash machine and how it works.

Book Link:
• *Dinosaurs to the Rescue* by Laurie Krasny Brown and Marc Brown (Joy Street Books, 1992).
This is a fun book about how to recycle and reuse materials. Dinosaurs, on each page, teach children many interesting facts about creating a clean and healthy planet. Children will learn how their televisions, Halloween costumes, and sand castles at the beach can help the environment!

TRASH MACHINES

LITTERBUGS

Teacher's Note:
Ask the children the question, "What is litter?" Litter is trash that people throw away, but not in a trash can. It usually lands on the ground! Ask, "Why is littering harmful?" It can be unsafe and makes the world an uglier place for everyone. Tell the children that a "litterbug" is someone who litters. Have them imagine what a litterbug might look like if it were truly a bug. Ask them, "What would it like to eat?" (Litter!)

Materials:
Paper cups and plates, cardboard tubes, aluminum foil, construction paper, cotton balls, straws, plastic utensils, ribbon, tape, glue

Directions:
1. Each child can make a litterbug by taping straws, cups, plates, and tubes together.
2. Children can use foil, cotton balls, construction paper, and ribbon to decorate their bugs.
3. When the bugs have dried, place them in a special area.
4. Give each bug a special award, such as: "The Hungriest-Looking Litterbug," "The Meanest-Looking Litterbug," or "The Silliest-Looking Litterbug."
5. The children can take their litterbugs home and use them as reminders not to litter!

Book Link:
• *World, World, What Can I Do?* by Barbara Shook Hazen (Morehouse, 1991).
This book offers fun rhymes as children show the world how they can take care of it. Each page shows a different type of environment that relates to each rhyme. Children can find out what they should do if they catch a firefly or climb a tree.

LITTERBUGS

MORE ECOLOGY RESOURCES FROM MONDAY MORNING BOOKS

Students will love exploring the natural world by making unique crafts, reading interesting literature links, conducting enlightening science experiments, and performing delightful shows. Each book contains a two-sided, four-color 17" x 22" poster bursting with environmental facts and information that children can understand. (For grades 1-3.)

Save the Animals! (MM 1964)
Students study endangered and extinct species while learning about animals they are more familiar with. Crafts include an endangered animal paper quilt—each child contributes a square.

Love the Earth! (MM 1965)
Children have an opportunity to visit environments all over the world through a variety of exciting projects. Locations include: deserts, oceans, rain forests, meadows, and cities.

Learn to Recycle! (MM 1966)
Can one person really make a difference when it comes to cleaning up the planet? Yes! And students learn how through a wide range of in-class and at-home projects. Children will help make their school, home, and world a cleaner place!